GOD IS A PERSON

DISCOVERING GOD FOR YOURSELF
WORKBOOK

Paul D. Nixon and Clarise Nixon

www.TrueVinePublishing.org

God is a Person: Discovering God for Yourself Workbook
Paul D. Nixon and Clarise Nixon

Published by True Vine Publishing Company
810 Dominican Dr.
Nashville TN. 37228
www.TrueVinePublishing.org

ISBN: 978-1-962783-05-7 Paperback
ISBN: 978-1-962783-13-2 eBook

Printed in the United States of America—First Printing

To order more books, for more information about the authors, or to book for speaking engagements, go to www.cpnix.com

Contents

INTRODUCTION

Welcome to the God Is a Person workbook! As you engage with this workbook, we want to encourage you to make the experience of the book more about your personal lifestyle. We've learned in academic settings that students tend not to make large-scale changes when those changes are informed by only one course or scattered experiences; they just want to complete the immediate task that's ahead of them and move on to the next task and, therefore, they aren't changed in significant ways.

Instead, large-scale changes are more likely to happen and remain when the experience is more immersive or campus-wide, when it is in their faces all the time. This workbook is designed to help you make the process of developing a real relationship with God a more immersive experience in your life so that you'll see the kinds of long-term changes you're looking for. It requires intentionality and consistency.

In this workbook, we have included a variety of practical activities. Some ask you to journal or write, some ask you to go out in nature and observe, some ask you to study a person from the Bible, and there are some activity challenges as well. We've provided some space for you to

"REFLECTING AND EVALUATING YOUR OWN PROCESS IS AN IMPORTANT STEP IN THE GROWTH OF A RELATIONSHIP."

write, but we encourage you to get a notebook or virtual journal if you want more space to write down your thoughts. Each practical activity also includes a QR code that will take you to a video with further explanation of the purpose of the activity.

Our intention here is to provide not only realistic exercises—things that you have the ability to do—but also practical exercises—things that you will actually do. You don't have to focus on every activity all the time, and you're free to skip over activities that aren't working for you—or even adapt them for smoother integration into your lifestyle. It's also okay if you have favorite steps that you want to keep returning to. Remember, the goal is to fit the activity into your life—not to do things just to say you did them.

Therefore, we also include blank lines for you to either write out the activity or reflect on your process as you grow with God. Reflecting and evaluating your own process is an important step in the growth of a relationship. It helps you to stay in tune with your progress and how you're adapting to this changing relationship. Write down questions, concerns, and joys that you want to share with God as you grow with Him. At the end of this workbook, we include helpful resources that we hope will guide you through knowing God better.

May God continue to bless you in your journey with Him!

Clarise and Paul Nixon
CP Nix

CH 1 - PRACTICAL STEPS FOR DISCOVERING THE ESSENCE OF GOD

God Is A Loving Person

1. Friendship Inventory

Think of God as a person with feelings and build a relationship with Him the way you would build a relationship with another person in your life.

Don't only focus on what you're getting out of the relationship, but pay attention to what you're giving to the relationship.

Write out answers to the following questions about your friends and apply the same questions to your relationship with God. Then, reflect on your answers and look for opportunities to build a more meaningful relationship with God:

a. What types of conversations do you have with your friends? What types of jokes do you tell?

b. What kinds of plans do you make with one another?

c. What emotions or stories do you share or keep to yourself?

d. In what ways do you show up for your friends when they need you?

> "DON'T ONLY FOCUS ON WHAT YOU'RE GETTING OUT OF THE RELATIONSHIP, BUT PAY ATTENTION TO WHAT YOU'RE GIVING TO THE RELATIONSHIP."

e. Do you participate in the same kinds of relationship building activities with God as you do with your friends?

_____

_____

_____

_____

_____

_____

_____

_____

_____

_____

_____

_____

_____

_____

_____

_____

"USE LOVE AS THE LENS THROUGH WHICH WE SEE GOD AND PERCEIVE HIS ACTIONS."

2. Listening During Prayer

Think of prayer as a time to listen and learn, not just to speak. Ask God to lay things on your heart that He wants to talk to you about that day.

Write out what God says to you during your listening session.

_____

_____

_____

_____

_____

_____

_____

_____

_____

_____

_____

3. Relationship-building Questions

Ask relationship-building questions of God and write out what you feel He is saying to you. Here are some examples:

How are You feeling?

How can I support Your kingdom and ultimate plan today?

What's my role in my relationship with You?

Do you want me to listen right now or respond?

_____

_____

_____

_____

_____

_____

_____

_____

_____

_____

_____

"GOD IS THE ULTIMATE SOURCE OF OTHER-CENTEREDNESS IN THE UNIVERSE, AND EVERYTHING HE DOES IS AN ACT OF LOVE."

4. 7-day Blessings Challenge

At the end of the day, take a slip of paper and write down one thing that God did for you that day. Place the slip of paper in a jar.

Do this every day for a week.

At the end of the week, empty the jar and, during your time with God, reflect on His love for you. Share with Him how His love for you makes you feel: grateful, loved, joyful, safe, etc.

There is no limit to how many slips you can write per day! Just be consistent for at least 7 days in a row and make sure each day you write at least 1 slip.

You can always return to this challenge whenever you doubt that God is a loving person, or when you struggle believing that He loves you specifically.

"FOCUS ON THE WAYS THAT GOD HAS DEMONSTRATED THAT HE LOVES YOU."

_____

_____

_____

_____

_____

_____

CH 2 - PRACTICAL STEPS FOR RIDICULOUS PRAYERS

God Is A Freeing Person

1. Planning Journal

Keep a Planning Journal as you make plans in different areas of your life and ask God to speak clearly to you whenever you're writing in it. Communicate with God first, before you start making plans, before you know what you want, before you are even totally clear on the options. This way you'll be planning with God as He's revealing Himself to you through the options that He shows you, through your desires, through Godly people who you ask for advice, etc. Spend time listening as well as writing and be intentional. Write out the plans you and God come up with together.

_____

_____

_____

_____

_____

"WHEN WE COOPERATE WITH GOD AND DO THINGS HIS WAY, WE CAN PARTICIPATE IN GOD'S FREEDOM AND BE COMPLETELY FREE."

2. Emotional Inventory

Use a mood tracker app to help you identify your emotional patterns; pay close attention to the emotional investment you have with your obstacles. Instead of investing in feelings like dread, worry, and stress, be open to reimagining problems as an opportunity for God to reveal Himself to you.

Be intentional about identifying fears in your prayers. What are you leaving out? What are you hiding from God? Kill the power of those fears by writing them out and praying about them specifically. Identify where and on what you spend most of your time. You have the ability to affect your emotions by what you spend your time doing in relation to your daily issues and problems. Make it a point to utilize this God-given ability to help you develop a healthier outlook.

Healthfully process (and move through) your emotions rather than planting yourself in them permanently. There's a difference between constantly rehearsing your problems (with friends, for example) and recognizing they exist while you bring them before God to see what He does with them.

"DISCOVER YOUR TRUE BASE EMOTIONS SO THAT THERE ARE NO EMOTIONAL BARRIERS BETWEEN YOU AND GOD."

Write out how your emotions change over time, how they affect your outlook and behavior, and how God has revealed Himself to you through this process.

Emotional Changes	Outlook or Behavioral Changes	God is...

3. Prayer List

Let God guide your prayer life. Use a prayer list that includes sections for:
- Intercession - add things that are focused on others
- Personal - add things that are focused on you
- Ridiculous - add things that should be impossible; things that only make sense through the power of Jesus Christ.

Intercession	Personal	Ridiculous

"COMMUNICATING WITH GOD THROUGH INTENTIONAL PRAYER IS LIKE HAVING AN INTIMATE CONVERSATION WITH GOD."

4. Bible Character Study

Study closely biblical characters who demonstrated full freedom in Christ such as Esther (in Esther), David (in 1 Samuel, 2 Samuel, and Psalms), Peter (in The Gospels, Acts, 1 Peter and 2 Peter), or Paul (in Acts or any of the Epistles that he authored).

In your character study, consider:
- How the character looks or presents themselves (appearance)
- How the character behaves (actions)
- How the character communicates, e.g. conversations, commands, sermons, songs, prayers, etc. (dialogue)
- How the character makes decisions (influences)
- What the character believes (thoughts and feelings)
- How & why the character repents (motives)

Take note of how they lived their lives (in their context) and think of ways you can follow those same principles in your own life (and in your own context).

Use the following pages to help you keep track of your thoughts. For multiple character studies, you can duplicate the chart in your notebook or virtual journal.

CHARACTERIZATION

Dialogue

_____
_____
_____
_____

Actions

_____
_____
_____
_____

Influences

_____
_____
_____
_____

Appearance

_____
_____
_____
_____

Thoughts & Feelings

_____
_____
_____
_____

character's name

ESTHER

cultural context _____

_____
_____
_____
_____
_____
_____
_____
_____
_____
_____
_____
_____
_____
_____
_____
_____
_____
_____
_____

_____
_____
_____
_____
_____
_____
_____
_____
_____
_____
_____
_____
_____
_____
_____
_____
_____
_____

CHARACTERIZATION

Dialogue
_____
_____
_____
_____

Actions
_____
_____
_____

Influences
_____
_____
_____

Appearance
_____
_____
_____

Thoughts & Feelings
_____
_____
_____

character's name   **DAVID**

cultural context   _____

CHARACTERIZATION

Dialogue

_____
_____
_____

Actions

_____
_____
_____
_____

Influences

_____
_____
_____
_____

Appearance

_____
_____
_____

Thoughts & Feelings

_____
_____
_____

character's name **PETER**

cultural context _____

_____
_____
_____
_____
_____
_____
_____
_____
_____
_____
_____
_____
_____
_____
_____
_____

JOURNAL

_____
_____
_____
_____
_____
_____
_____
_____
_____
_____
_____
_____
_____
_____
_____
_____
_____
_____

CHARACTERIZATION

Dialogue
_____
_____
_____

Actions
_____
_____
_____

Influences
_____
_____
_____

Appearance
_____
_____
_____

Thoughts & Feelings
_____
_____
_____

character's name   PAUL

cultural context   _____

5. How to Know God's Will Challenge

Choose a decision with which you're struggling for this particular challenge as you seek clarity and guidance. As you seek God's will, write down your reflections, answers to prayers, changes in your desires or plans, etc.

Keep in mind that this challenge could take a number of days, but don't be discouraged! We recommend taking at least 5-7 days to complete it, but remember that it could take longer than that! Remain spiritually curious during this process and get excited about what God is going to reveal to you in His time.

"GET PRACTICAL WITH GOD... IF YOU ARE CONSIDERING A MAJOR PURCHASE OR CHANGE IN JOB, THIS 7-DAY CHALLENGE IS FOR YOU."

Part 1 - Surrender your will (John 5:30)

First, you have to be honest with yourself and acknowledge what you want, even if it's petty or shallow. Tell God the truth about yourself—He knows it anyway!

Once you're honest about what you want, determine that you are willing to do what God wants you to do, even if it's not what you want. You won't be able to hear God's voice if you are dedicated to getting what you want.

Write out what you want out of the situation and what you don't want. If you're unsure of what you want, write out a pros and cons list.

What I Want (Pros)	What I Don't Want (Cons)

Part 2 - Pray about it (Matthew 7:7-8)

Ask God in prayer to reveal His will to you in ways that you will be able to understand and write out what He reveals.

Don't just speak during prayer, but listen also. Be sensitive to the influence of the Holy Spirit. Remember that the main purpose of prayer is to bring our hearts into harmony with God's heart, so that we may receive His answers to our prayers.

Part 3 - Search the scriptures (Psalm 119:105)

Sometimes the answer to your question will be found in the precise words of a Bible text. Other times, the answer will be in a biblical principle. Remember that God will never direct you to do something that is contrary to His Word or His already-revealed will. Write out Bible texts that are relevant to your situation as you discover them.

Don't just read the Bible to look for texts that agree with you, but rather study the Bible, including the context of the verses you're reading, for light from the Lord on the issue you're praying about.

Part 4 - Look for the providential circumstance (Genesis 24:10-27)

Ask God to use your circumstances to speak to you. There may be a situation—beyond your control but natural to your circumstances—that God can use to indicate His will for your life. But be careful! Don't make up some bizarre test for God to complete like, "If this is Your will, send a bee to fly by my head right now." Be led by inspiration as God directs you.

In the Genesis 24 example, the servant's prayer test involved another person God could use to communicate His message. It wasn't something random like "whether or not a humming bird lands on this leaf."

Write out your prayer test and how God responds to it.

_____

_____

_____

_____

_____

_____

_____

_____

_____

_____

_____

_____

Part 5 - Consult Godly friends (Proverbs 11:14)

Ask someone in your life who has a relationship with God for their opinion on the situation. Remember that you do not have to face this situation alone! This is especially important to remember when making decisions that you have strong feelings about. Your own emotions may blind you to things that are important to consider. Try not to be stubborn. Take advantage of the wisdom from the spiritually mature people in your life.

Remember to consult *Godly* people, not necessarily the people who are closest to you. This isn't just a matter of asking another person their opinion. It's important to consult people who are themselves connected to God.

Write out who you talk to and their response to your situation.

Part 6 - Exercise patience (Psalm 27:14; Habakkuk 2:3)

At this point in the process, you may be getting impatient, thinking you should know by now. It can be very difficult to wait on the Lord, yet patience is a required discipline for anyone who wants to truly follow God. Remember that God doesn't operate on our timetable; it's important that we learn to operate on His. So as long as God's will is unclear on this issue, don't decide anything yet!

It's possible that God doesn't want you to make a change at all. Or maybe you are not yet ready to receive what God intends for you. Remember that God's view is infinitely greater than ours and that God is interested in much more than just this one isolated decision for your life, even if it's a huge decision in your eyes.

Write out the actions you are taking to remain patient during this process.

_____

_____

_____

_____

_____

_____

_____

_____

_____

_____

Part 7 - When God does speak, obey and act! (Hebrews 11:8)

Once God has clearly revealed His will to you, stop waiting! Obey Him without delay. Do not consult anyone after God's will is clear to you. Trust in God and believe His promise to take care of you. You should inform people of any major changes in your life, but stop asking for other opinions once you're clear on God's will.

Ask the Lord to confirm your decision as you carry it out by opening the doors before you. You will gain confidence as you see circumstances arranged to enable you to do God's will. Your faith in God will deepen and your commitment to God will strengthen. And, it will be easier to complete this challenge the next time you face a major decision!

Write out God's revealed will below. What actions will you take to move forward?

_____

_____

_____

_____

_____

_____

_____

_____

_____

_____

CH 3 - PRACTICAL STEPS FOR CHRISTIAN ARTISTRY

God Is A Creative Person

1. Submit Your Preferences to God

Take some time to decide what you really want for yourself. What are your biggest goals for your talents? Admit that you have preferences and desires of your own. Then, pray to God and ask Him to do what He wants to do with you, even if it means not getting the thing that you most want from your talents.

Remember that there is nothing wrong with having a preference, or with wanting things for yourself. The problem many of us have is not that we want things, it's that we ignore the voice and direction of God in our pursuit of the things we want. We must train ourselves to obey God even when obeying Him doesn't take us through the path we prefer or lead us to our preferred final destination.

Write out your preferences below and name each one specifically in prayer.

"ACCEPT WHAT GOD WANTS FOR YOU, EVEN IF IT IS DIFFERENT FROM WHAT YOU WANT FOR YOURSELF."

2. Target Practice

Ask God to reveal a specific person or group that He wants to target with your talents, even if it's with people you don't already have a close relationship with.

This is a great opportunity to practice sacrificial giving. Give to your target group or person at a discounted rate or even without charging them. And give your best work! Don't merely donate the throwaway stuff that you would never sell anyway, for example.

Use this as an opportunity to make connections with people and write out below the connections you make by allowing God to choose your target audience.

_____

_____

_____

_____

_____

_____

_____

_____

_____

"GOD'S CREATIVITY IS ON FULL DISPLAY IN OUR LIVES... USE YOUR CREATIVITY FOR GOD'S GLORY... "

> "GET OUT OF YOUR OWN WAY... DELIGHT IN THE FACT THAT GOD SEES VALUE IN WHAT YOU HAVE TO OFFER AND HIS TIMING IS DIFFERENT THAN OUR OWN."

3. Baby Steps

Sometimes major goals can feel daunting because of what they require. To help you reach your goals, fill out the The Path Forward form, taking note of the major goal you want to reach and the smaller steps that will get you there. No step is too small to list if the step moves you closer to your major goal!

Keep in mind that with any process, there will be failures along the way; it's important to assess your emotions: are you feeling empowered or discouraged? Like you're moving forward or are immobile? What lessons are you learning that you can apply right away?

When you complete a baby step, check it off and celebrate! Achieving your major goals one step at a time will keep you focused, encourage you along the way and give you smaller, but vital, milestones to celebrate.

If it seems to be taking a long time to reach your major goal, focus on the path, not the destination. This might seem counter-intuitive, but sometimes focusing on the goal can be disheartening because the goal seems so far away. Instead, focus on the step you are on in the process, or the next step you have to take. Turn your attention to the smaller thing, and note that baby steps are still steps.

If the steps you are taking are within God's will, the destination will take care of itself. Pray for the strength to be obedient to God's will every day—or even several times a day—and follow through.

The Path Forward form begins on the next page!

The Path Forward

Major goal (be as precise as possible):

_____

_____

By when do you hope to accomplish this goal?

_____

What smaller, baby steps are necessary for you to reach this goal? How long do you anticipate each of these steps taking? How are you feeling along the way? What lessons can you apply?

Baby Step 1: _____

Duration: _____

While achieving this step, I feel

_____

One lesson I learned during this step is

_____

Baby Step 2: _____

Duration: _____

While achieving this step, I feel

_____

One lesson I learned during this step is

_____

Baby Step 3: _____

Duration: _____

While achieving this step, I feel

_____

One lesson I learned during this step is

_____

Baby Step 4: _____

Duration: _____

While achieving this step, I feel

_____

One lesson I learned during this step is

_____

Baby Step 5: _____

Duration: _____

While achieving this step, I feel

_____

One lesson I learned during this step is

_____

4. Vertical vs Horizontal Comparisons

Comparing yourself to other people (horizontal comparisons) can easily take your focus off of God and what His purpose is for you. This shift in focus can lead to discouragement and even depression, which can stifle artistry and creativity.

During your creative activities, try to refocus your attention on God (vertical comparisons) and away from other people as often as you need to by answering the following questions:

What purpose does God have for me during this journey?

_____

_____

_____

_____

_____

_____

_____

_____

_____

"SQUELCH THE POWER OF UNHEALTHY COMPARISONS... COMPARE YOURSELF TO GOD'S EXPECTATION AND STANDARD FOR YOU."

What skills and/or personality traits has He given me that make me a unique fit for this purpose?

_____

_____

What has He done so far that tells me He's with me and He sees me?

_____

_____

What hasn't happened that could have happened to destroy my progress?

_____

_____

How can I partner with people God has placed in my life?

_____

_____

How can I be of service to someone else who might be discouraged?

_____

_____

Bonus: You can also return to The Path Forward form if you filled one out. What have you accomplished so far? Celebrate the ways God has helped you with the little wins, and keep pushing!

5. Nature Challenge

Take a morning or an afternoon and find a place outside where you have a good view of nature, whether that means a park, the beach, or even your own front porch.

Be deliberate about observing nature through your five senses—write down what you see, smell, feel, taste, and hear. Can you taste anything in the air? Write it down. What elements do you feel? Write them down in the table below.

Spend time focusing on each sense and recognizing that all of these sensations were naturally and intentionally created by God for your enjoyment. What spiritual applications do you see in nature? Write out any spiritual applications that you come up with on the following page.

"DISCOVER GOD'S CREATIVITY IN NATURE... TAKE SOME TIME TO THANK GOD FOR THE MAJESTY OF HIS CREATION."

Sight	Sound	Smell	Touch	Taste

Spiritual Applications

> "TAP INTO GOD'S IDEA OF FUN...IMAGINE GOD AS A FUN-LOVING PERSON."

CH 4 - PRACTICAL STEPS FOR FUN IN GOD'S WILL

God Is A Fun-loving Person

1. List of Fun Things

Here is a short 3-step process to help you to find the fun in God's will for your life. As always, honesty is key to this exercise because it will unlock the full potential of this activity. Make a list of some of the things that you enjoy doing, whether they are things that you actually get a chance to do, or things that you wish you could do more often. The list is not so much about what you actually do, it is more about what you like to do. So feel free to include things on the list that you do rarely, but that you do when you can because you enjoy doing them.

Once your list is complete, prayerfully go through the activities one by one and determine if that activity is an accurate reflection of the character of Jesus Christ. Does your involvement in the activity draw you closer to God, or does it push you further away? You may need help with this step, and if you do, we encourage you to involve your spouse, your best friend, your closest sibling, or your counselor. Run your ideas by another Christian person who has a similar value system to you and who will tell you the truth.

Write your insights below.

For every activity you identify that is questionable or is clearly not something God is happy with, pray for deliverance from it. If you stop engaging in that activity, that is very good; if you stop wanting to engage in that activity, that is even better. If you replace that activity with something that is in God's will, that is best. Ask God to change your desires so that you only want to do what He wants you to do. And ask Him to not only give you the sense of fun that you sincerely desire, but to attach that feeling of fun to the things He wants for you. Write down what activities you need to stop or approach differently and what you're going to do differently.

_____

_____

_____

_____

_____

_____

_____

_____

_____

_____

_____

2. Nature Group Activity
(This practical step does not have a video.)

Organize or participate in a group activity in nature, such as going to the beach, having a picnic, going on a hike, or going to a park. Do something outside your home with a group of people that you like, or a group of people that you want to get to know better.

Make this activity about focusing on Christ or on others. Try some of these ideas:

Invite people that are outside of your inner circle to join you on a hike.

Bring extra food with you on your picnic to give away to someone you encounter or invite them to join you.

Go to your local park and bring some bottles of water with you to distribute to people playing sports.

By focusing our attention on other people during a fun activity, we will be both having fun and getting closer to God at the same time.

3. Focus on the Message

(This practical step does not have a video.)

If it's true that our bodies are the temple of God, then that must include our brains; we are responsible for being good stewards of our minds. This means that we should exercise our intellect just like we exercise our bodies, and we can have fun in the process!

Watch a Christian movie that you expect to be poorly produced and find a way to focus on the positive message of the movie anyway. Building this intellectual skill at home can help you demonstrate it in other settings.

Several digital platforms have a wide selection of positive motivational or Christian films that are not really executed well. They have stories with huge plot holes, bad acting, cheap production value, and novice directing, but their message is focused on Christ. Even these films, however, have value.

To help keep your focus, you might make a game out of it.

Challenge a group of friends to see who can list the most biblical principles that are in the movie you're watching.

At the end, compare your lists and cross out ones that are duplicated among the group. The person with the most biblical principles that haven't been crossed out wins (sort of like the game Scattergories).

Afterward, have a friendly discussion about the positive themes or biblical principles you've listed and how you can include them in your life in practical, realistic ways. Use the space below to record your experience with this activity.

4. New Habit Challenge

Research shows that successfully stopping a bad habit doesn't just automatically happen; instead, you need to replace your bad habits with healthier, new ones. This challenge is designed to help you identify a specific fun habit that you have that isn't in God's will and to replace it with something fun that is in God's will.

First, complete practical step 1 from this chapter. Practical step 1 is meant to help you find something you do for fun that isn't in God's will. We'll call it "old fun" for the purpose of this exercise. Once you know what old fun is for you, proceed with this challenge.

What triggers old fun for you? Make it harder to have old fun by identifying and eliminating the trigger. For example, if you watch too much television, put the remote control in an inconvenient place, like the closet in another room, or consider taking the TV out of your bedroom so you aren't tempted to have it on all night long. Write out what your old fun is and what your triggers are.

"IDENTIFY SPECIFIC FUN THAT YOU HAVE THAT IS NOT WITHIN GOD'S WILL, AND REPLACE IT WITH FUN THAT IS WITHIN GOD'S WILL."

This is really important: choose a specific, fun, Christ-centered activity to do whenever you have the urge for old fun; we'll call this new activity (wait for it....) "new fun." To achieve sustained success you can't just let something go, you have to do something else instead. If you're trying to watch less television, and you like the outdoors, maybe go for a walk or a bike ride during some of your normal TV watching time.

It's also important that the new fun activity is actually fun for you! Don't try to replace watching TV with reading if you hate reading. This isn't about doing "the right thing"; it's about continuing to have fun in your life, but cooperating with the Holy Spirit more fully as you do so. Write out your new fun activity and how it's going to replace the old fun activity.

Select an accountability partner. This needs to be a person whom you trust to check on your progress without making you feel worse about yourself. Maybe you can offer to provide the same support for them— you check on some goal they have for themselves and they check on your New Habit Challenge. Make a pact with your accountability partner to always be honest and encouraging with each other about reaching your goals. And remember, this is 100% a Judgment-Free Zone.

Accountability Partner:

_____

_____

What qualities make this person a good accountability partner?

_____

_____

_____

_____

Take small steps. If your goal is to watch less TV, don't try to cut out all TV at once. Instead, reduce your TV watching a little at a time as you increase the length of your walks or your bike rides.

Plan for failure. Building new habits is really difficult, so be gracious with yourself. If you fall short of your goal on a particular day, remember that tomorrow is another day and you will do better next time. Use "but" statements when you talk about your failure to reach your goal: "I watched 4 hours of TV today and didn't take a walk, but, tomorrow my goal is to only watch 3 1/2 hours of TV and walk for 30 minutes." When you fail, promise yourself to do better next time, and pray for the strength to keep your promise. Document your progress.

Celebrate success! Be grateful to God for progress that you make, and allow yourself to feel good about it. You can even plan a small celebration at certain milestones. For example, if you consistently reduce your TV watching by 30 minutes and replace that time with outdoor activities, you might buy yourself a new pair of walking sneakers to celebrate. Write out ideas for small celebrations that you can look forward to as you engage in this challenge.

Whatever your old fun, your new fun and your celebrations, remember that the point of all of this is to continue to have fun. Don't replace old fun with some chore, and don't celebrate with something you don't actually like. Have fun in God's will!

"CONFRONT PAIN THAT YOU ARE STILL HOLDING ON TO...PRAY FOR THE DESIRE TO EVEN WANT TO FORGIVE."

CH 5 - PRACTICAL STEPS FOR SPIRITUAL DIALYSIS

God Is A Community-minded Person

1. The Healing Path

Pray about how you can regain or create love for a community that has hurt, ignored, or neglected you. Identify the community you're focusing on and your ideas for reconnection below.

Community	Reconnection

2. Bible Study

Study Isaiah 1:1-17. From these verses, write a list of offenses the church in Isaiah's day did wrong and God's intention for the church.

Compare this list to your own church life. What are specific areas of your church life that you can improve?

Ancient Offenses	Modern Improvements

"RECOGNIZE THAT PEOPLE OF GOD HAVE BEEN HURTING GOD FOR THOUSANDS OF YEARS."

> "TAKE OWNERSHIP OF THE COMMUNITY YOU ARE A PART OF...IF YOU ARE A GOD-FEARING PERSON, SHINE YOUR LIGHT WHERE YOU ARE."

3. Fight For Your Community

If your church is distorting the image of God through its practices, fight for it instead of leaving. Because the church is the body of Christ, the reputation of the church and, therefore, Christ's reputation, is on the line.

You don't always have to reinvent the wheel; find an organization in your community that is doing necessary work and add your passion to their cause by making intentional connections with them and your church. Be an instrumental piece of the puzzle that helps get your church back on track in God's will.

4. Journal Prompt

Make 2 lists: one that focuses on explicit reasons why you want to leave (or have already left) your church (e.g., the pain/trauma you experienced) and another list that focuses on what God is revealing through the Bible and communion with Him about your situation. What are God's specific instructions to you?

Study the following passages/characters as you search for answers and record your findings on the following page.

- Is God permitting you to leave? Read Acts 15, which highlights a situation that leads fellow believers to "agree to disagree" and part ways while still continuing their spiritual journeys.
- Is God allowing you to take a short break? During Jesus' ministry, He often left the toxic environment around Him to refresh Himself, but always came back to the community to continue His mission.
  ◊ Luke 22:39-44 - Jesus prays on the Mount of Olives
  ◊ Luke 5:16 - Jesus withdraws to pray
  ◊ Matthew 14:1-13 - Jesus withdraws to grieve
  ◊ Mark 6:30-32 - Jesus leads the disciples to rest after their ministry tour

"DECIDE HOW TO REACT WHEN YOU EXPERIENCE TROUBLE OR PAIN FROM YOUR CHURCH COMMUNITY."

- Is God requiring you to stay where you are?
  - ◊ Hosea 1-3 - Hosea called to marry a prostitute
  - ◊ Jeremiah 20 - Jeremiah in prison
- Is God asking you to go somewhere you don't want to go?
  - ◊ Exodus 3 - God's call to Moses
  - ◊ Jonah 1-3 - Jonah called to Nineveh

Why Do You Want to Leave?	What is God Revealing?

5. Start A _____ Challenge

This challenge is meant to help you identify a need around you—in your society, at work, in your neighborhood, somewhere else. Start to attend to that need in a small way and build from there.

- Week 1: Address the problem on your own in some small way when you see it. For example, if you see a need for your neighborhood to be more clean and you see a piece of trash on the ground, (grab a disposable glove and) pick it up and throw it away.
- Week 2: Invite your friends to join you in your activity.
- Week 3: Ask your friends to each invite another person to join the group so that you start to build a larger community.

Remember these two things: addressing something all the time doesn't necessarily mean it'll go away. There might always be trash to pick up, but the point is you're picking it up instead of looking to someone else to pick it up.

Also remember to plan for success. If this really starts to build and get popular, before you know it, you could

"IDENTIFY A NEED AROUND YOU AND START ATTENDING TO THAT NEED IN YOUR COMMUNITY."

be managing events and dozens of people. Don't be fearful! Instead, as your community builds, pray for a team to also form. A planner, a graphic designer, someone with equipment or a large network, financial advisors, or anyone else you need to continue your project. Write down the progress you start to see below and how your initial small efforts are growing larger every week.

CH 6 - PRACTICAL STEPS FOR UNDERSTANDING GOD'S SOVEREIGNTY

God Is A Supreme Person

1. Journal Prompt

What is your true motivation for following Christ? What if there were no heaven? Would you still want to be His follower and His friend? Are you primarily following Him because of the relationship or because of the rewards? Reflect on these questions in writing.

"THINK REALISTICALLY ABOUT WHAT YOUR TRUE MOTIVATIONS ARE FOR FOLLOWING GOD."

_____

_____

_____

_____

_____

_____

_____

_____

_____

_____

_____

> "DO A DEEP-DIVE INTO CHARACTERS OF THE BIBLE...THE BIBLE ISN'T THE STORY OF WHAT HUMAN BEINGS DID, IT'S A STORY OF WHAT GOD DID FOR HUMAN BEINGS."

2. Biblical Character Study

Using the templates on the next pages, perform a character study of Samson (Judges chs. 13-16), Ruth (Ruth chs. 1-4), Daniel (Daniel chs. 9-10), and Jonah (Jonah chs. 1-4), using the following questions as a guide:

- What was their attitude during their hardships?
- How does God demonstrate grace in these people's lives?
- How does God show His sovereignty in these stories?

Use the next few pages to help keep track of your thoughts.

CHARACTERIZATION

Attitude

_____
_____
_____
_____
_____
_____
_____

God's Grace

_____
_____
_____
_____
_____
_____
_____
_____

God's Sovereignty

_____
_____
_____
_____
_____
_____
_____

character's name **SAMSON**

cultural context _____

_____
_____
_____
_____
_____
_____
_____
_____
_____
_____
_____
_____
_____
_____
_____
_____
_____
_____

_____
_____
_____
_____
_____
_____
_____
_____
_____
_____
_____
_____
_____
_____
_____
_____
_____

CHARACTERIZATION

Attitude

_____
_____
_____
_____
_____
_____

God's Grace

_____
_____
_____
_____
_____
_____

God's Sovereignty

_____
_____
_____
_____

character's name

cultural context

RUTH

CHARACTERIZATION

Attitude

_____
_____
_____
_____
_____
_____
_____

God's Grace

_____
_____
_____
_____
_____
_____
_____
_____

God's Sovereignty

_____
_____
_____
_____
_____
_____
_____

DANIEL

character's name

cultural context _____

_____
_____
_____
_____
_____
_____
_____
_____
_____
_____
_____
_____
_____
_____
_____
_____
_____

JOURNAL

_____
_____
_____
_____
_____
_____
_____
_____
_____
_____
_____
_____
_____
_____
_____
_____
_____
_____

CHARACTERIZATION

Attitude

_____
_____
_____
_____
_____
_____
_____

God's Grace

_____
_____
_____
_____
_____
_____
_____
_____

God's Sovereignty

_____
_____
_____
_____
_____

character's name **JONAH**

cultural context _____

3. Personal Reflection

Evaluate and/or reflect on a particularly difficult situation or time in your life. Discuss with a trusted friend how God demonstrated grace and sovereignty during this time. Record your thoughts below.

"LOOK AT A TROUBLING SITUATION FROM A DIFFERENT POINT OF VIEW... SOMETIMES A BAD SITUATION IS SAFETY FROM A WORSE SITUATION."

_____

_____

_____

_____

_____

_____

_____

_____

_____

_____

_____

_____

_____

_____

_____

"BUILD YOUR TRUST IN GOD AND RELY MORE FULLY ON HIS SOVEREIGNTY."

4. Trust in God Challenge

Part 1 - Remind Yourself of God's Goodness & Remember that He is in Control

Every day, remind yourself of something God did for you that was good. This sounds simple, but there are some things that can make this more challenging. If you had a particularly bad day, it might be hard to find God's goodness in it. Also, if you accomplish something great, it might be easy to take credit for it instead of seeing God's goodness in your success. Whether things are going great or you're barely hanging on, remind yourself that God's goodness is not dependent on your circumstances.

Also remember that a relationship with any person means relying on the other person at times, even when it's not comfortable. A relationship with God is similar, except God is completely reliable, and He is in control. So, remind yourself that God is actually the one in control and He is looking out for you all the time. Record your thoughts on the next page.

Once you've made it a habit to focus on something good that God did for you every day, move to Part 2.

Part 2 - Focus on God's Character

Pay particular attention to one aspect of God's character, and look for examples of His character in your everyday life. Some examples of God's character include:

- Infinite (Colossians 1:17)
- Consistent (Malachi 3:6)
- Self-Sufficient (John 5:26)
- Loving (1 John 4:7-8)
- Kind (Psalm 34:8)
- Faithful (Deuteronomy 7:9)
- Merciful (Romans 9:15-16)
- Gracious (Psalm 145:8)

- Holy (Revelation 4:8)
- Glorious (Habakkuk 3:4)
- Just (Deuteronomy 32:4)
- Wise (Romans 11:33)
- Omniscient (Isaiah 46:9-10)
- Omnipresent (Jeremiah 23:23-34)
- Omnipotent (Job 11:7-11)

Zoom in on any one aspect of God's character. Try to understand what it means, and then dedicate some of your attention to seeing that aspect of God in your environment. Record your thoughts. Once you are reassured that God is in fact who He says he is, move on to Part 3.

Part 3 - Pray to Grow Your Faith

When you have clarity on who God is, you can begin to approach Him differently.

- God is King of the Universe, so He is supremely elevated.
- He is also the Leader of the Armies of Heaven, so He is supremely powerful.
- And He is a friend to human beings, so He is supremely approachable.
- Because of all of this, He is supremely trustworthy.

Start to approach Christ in prayer with this assurance: He is an elevated, powerful leader who you can put your complete trust in, and He is your friend. Record your reflections on your new approach to God.

Once you feel like you are beginning to trust God more, move on to Part 4.

Part 4 - Study God's Word & Listen for His Voice

The Bible is the living, active Word of God. Once you begin to realize that God is who He says He is, you should spend some time getting to know who He is even better by studying the Bible. Notice we didn't say *reading* the Bible; we said *studying* the Bible. There's a major difference here.

You might read a magazine or a newspaper article; you might read your favorite novel or the subtitles of a foreign film. These are things you would read, but they aren't necessarily things you would study. Study involves reading and analyzing, considering the background and context of what you're reading, and making sure you understand what you're reading before moving on to the next thing. We recommend using a good study Bible for this purpose.

A good study Bible can help a lot with turning your Bible reading into Bible studying by helping you to look deeper at what the text is trying to teach you. We also recommend following the tips that are listed on the next page whenever you study your Bible; this process can really open up the Word of God in ways you may have never experienced before.

Don't be ashamed to spend a short period of time on this at first. Thirty minutes per day is a lot compared with nothing at all! The goal here is not to become a Bible scholar; it's to get to know God better so you can trust Him more.

- Ask the Holy Spirit to give you guidance before you even start reading; some spiritual truths will only be recognized through God revealing them to you (1 Corinthians 2:14).

- Read your verse in at least 3 versions (compare/contrast words, phrases).

- Close read: list important concepts, create summary statements of what you understand the text means.

- Read the surrounding section and chapter to get a better idea of the context of the verses you're studying.

- Take note of the historical context: politically, socially, philosophically, and economically (your study Bible will help). Sometimes it helps to watch supplemental videos that simply and clearly explain these kinds of contexts; we highly recommend The Bible Project channel on YouTube. Write notes of what you're studying and any insights you make.

Listening to God involves spending quiet time during prayer when you're not actually saying anything, but you're listening for God's voice. It also involves searching the scriptures to hear God's voice and recognizing His character through His word. If you're going to build a relationship with God, you must not only bring Him your concerns and desires, but you must also listen to His concerns and desires. Relationships are a 2-way street, and so is your relationship with God. Write out what God reveals to you in prayer below.

Once you have made listening to God a part of your prayer and Bible study routine, move to Part 5.

Part 5 - Follow God

Now that you know who God is, you can trust that He is looking out for you. You realize He is in control and you have begun to make consistent use of your direct access to Him. The last step can sometimes be the hardest: be obedient, and do what He says.

Obedience looks different for every person. For you it might mean leaving your job that you love, or staying in your job that you don't really like. It could be doubling down on a commitment you made when you were considering giving it up, or leaving a situation that has grown unhealthy. Whatever it is specifically for you, the common thread is that you are letting God guide your decision instead of relying on your impulses, emotions, or intellect. This is the essence of trust and obedience. Follow God and watch Him take care of the details! Write out how you're being obedient to God below.

_____

_____

_____

_____

_____

_____

_____

_____

_____

_____

_____

CH 7 - PRACTICAL STEPS FOR FOCUSING ON GOD

God Is An Attentive Person

1. Cultivate Stillness and Quiet

Make it a point to gather at least a few minutes each day to be still and quiet. Spend those minutes in close, personal fellowship with God.

Give God your full attention; be mindful of His presence. Put a reminder in your calendar for this to help you be intentional, and then silence your cell phone, turn off the TV, and go to a quiet place. Document how many minutes during a particular time of day that you spend in quiet time with God, and write out what you hear God saying to you during your quiet time.

"PRACTICE MINDFULNESS WITH GOD. GOD USUALLY SPEAKS QUIETLY. IT CAN BE DIFFICULT TO HEAR HIM IF OUR MINDS ARE CONSTANTLY RINGING IN OUR EARS."

Time of Day	Minutes in Quiet	Message

2. Seek God First

Pastor Craig Groeschel of Life.Church encourages his congregants with this activity.

Make a list of the positive characteristics that God placed in you, and find accompanying Bible verses that build your confidence in those characteristics.

Instead of beginning your day by checking social media or the news, begin by reading your list aloud to yourself.

Start the day by posturing your heart before God, focusing your mind on biblical truths and making every thought captive to the will of Christ (2 Corinthians 10:5).

Below is an example of a list of biblical truths that you can speak aloud to refocus and, therefore, renew your mind every day.

"BEGIN THE DAY BY INTENTIONALLY FOCUSING YOUR THOUGHTS TOWARDS GOD."

Words to Live By Example

"I am named by God, not labeled by man. I will walk in the truth of who God says I am."

- I am a child of God. (Galatians 3:26)
- I am content with Christ alone. (Psalms 73:26)

- I am joyful. I am gentle. I am self-controlled. I am patient. (Galatians 5:22-23)
- I am creative, and I will use my creativity to serve God. (Exodus 35:34-35, Colossians 3:23-24)
- I am courageous & self-disciplined. (II Timothy 1:7)
- I am empathetic. (Romans 12:15)
- I am loved. (John 3:16)
- The joy of the Lord is my strength. (Nehemiah 8:10)
- God always provides a way out of temptation, and I will look for, recognize, and take it. (1 Corinthians 10:13)
- He will help me; I only need to ask. (Matthew 7:7)
- God meets my needs. (Philippians 4:19)
- I submit to God and resist the devil. (James 4:7)
- I fight for purity, guarding my eyes and heart from tempting situations. (Romans 8:5-6)
- Nothing can separate me from God. (Romans 8:38-39)
- Sin has no power over me. (Romans 6:14)
- I have authority over the devil and I can resist him through Christ. (Luke 10:19; James 4:7)
- I have the mind of Christ. (1 Corinthians 2:16; Philippians 4:8)
- I am not defined by what I have done. Greater is He that lives in me than he that lives in the world. (1 John 4:4)
- My record has been wiped clean. (Psalm 103:12)
- You are my God who keeps His word. You are faithful throughout all the generations. (Psalm 119:90)

Write your own Words to Live By list on the lines below.

FOLLOW 3 SIMPLE STEPS FOR CREATING YOUR OWN WORDS TO LIVE BY LIST HERE.

> "TAKE BACK YOUR OWN ATTENTION... WHEN YOU REMOVE SOMETHING FROM YOUR LIFE, YOU MUST REPLACE IT WITH SOMETHING BETTER."

3. Reduce Your Exposure to Media

This challenge is designed to give your mind a break from media so that you can focus more on growing closer with God.

Part 1 - Media Inventory

Take a quick inventory of how much time each day you spend on certain types of media—whether it's social media, the news, video games, or TV and movies—and the time of day you engage with that media.

Media Type	Time Spent	Time of Day

Part 2 - Take a Break!

Every day for 7 straight days, do not engage with that media at all. Choose one media type to take a break from for all 7 days, or you can choose a different media type each day to take a break from. What we don't recommend is replacing one type of media with another one. In other words, don't take a break from social media and instead watch more TV. The overall goal here is to reduce how much time you're spending with media of all kinds and fill that time with something else—journaling, focusing on family time, creating in God, reading, etc. Record your experience below.

"TAKE A BREAK FROM MEDIA IN ORDER TO GROW CLOSER TO GOD..."

_____

_____

_____

_____

_____

_____

_____

_____

_____

Part 3 - Freewrite

At the end of the seven days, do 7 minutes of freewriting on your experience. When you freewrite, the most important rule to remember is don't stop writing. Set a timer for 7 minutes and don't stop writing about what the last 7 days have been like for you and what challenges and benefits you experienced by taking a break from media. We recommend doing this free writing exercise by hand, but it can work well if you're typing it, too. When you write, don't focus on any writing mistakes that you make—typos, misspelled words, and poor punctuation are all welcome, so don't let those kinds of mistakes distract you.

Part 4 - Evaluate

When you're finished freewriting, look over what you wrote and appreciate that you successfully completed a difficult task. Record your takeaways from this experience below.

_____

_____

_____

_____

_____

_____

_____

_____

_____

_____

_____

_____

_____

_____

_____

_____

_____

4. Protagonist Challenge

(This practical step does not have a video.)

Discovering the guiding principle in your life can sometimes be very difficult. It requires a level of transparency, honesty, and critical thinking that doesn't come easy.

This challenge is designed to help you discover the main character in your life. The goal is not to judge your motives, just to identify them. At the end of the challenge, the goal is not just self-awareness, but also confidence in the ability to make God the main character in your life.

Part 1 - Discovery

Evaluate how you make your decisions, whether they are major life decisions or smaller, daily decisions. What is the underlying goal of what you are trying to achieve? What outside influences affect your thinking and, therefore, your desires? What factors do you see yourself ignoring during your decision-making processes? What factors do you gravitate toward during your decision-making processes?

For example, you might think about finances in your decisions, or what's best for your family, or how your decisions will affect your reputation or comfort level. Try to dig deep and get to the root of your motives. Record your thoughts.

Part 2 - Name Your Protagonist(s)

Based on what you discovered in Part 1, look for common threads or themes in your thinking. The goal here is to zero-in on a specific term that represents the protagonist that guides your decision-making. For example, if you discovered that money is often on your mind when you're making decisions, "financial security" or "generational wealth," might be a guiding principle. Or, if you discovered that comfort is often on your mind when you're making decisions, "comfort" might be a guiding principle. If service heavily influences your thinking, "service" might be a guiding principle.

Write out your guiding principles.

Guiding Principle 1
_____

Guiding Principle 2
_____

Guiding Principle 3
_____

Guiding Principle 4
_____

Guiding Principle 5
_____

Part 3 - Logic of _____

The goal of this activity is to analyze the logic behind the guiding principles in your life. This analysis will lead to further discovery and will help you decide if and how the protagonist in your life needs to change.

Choose 1 guiding principle to focus on at a time and write your principle in the blank next to "Logic of." Then, fill out the "Logic of" form, thinking through the 8 components of rational thought as outlined by Dr. Richard Paul, founder of the Foundation for Critical Thinking, and educational psychologist Dr. Linda Elder.

Logic of _____
(place your guiding principle on the line above)

1. What is the purpose of your guiding principle?

_____

_____

(Here, you are trying to state, as accurately as possible, your intent; what are you trying to accomplish with this guiding principle?)

2. What are the main questions being addressed within your guiding principle? What are the main problems being addressed?

_____

_____

(Your goal here is to figure out the key question that's in your mind with the guiding principle; what question do you hope your guiding principle will answer?)

3. What are the main assumptions being made about your guiding principle?

_____

_____

(Ask yourself: "What am I taking for granted that might be questioned?"Assumptions are generalizations that you don't think you need to defend within your context.)

4. What are the main implications and consequences of your guiding principle? What follows from it logically?

_____

_____

(What is likely to follow if your guiding principle is fulfilled? If it isn't fulfilled?)

5. What conclusions are you drawing about your guiding principle? What inferences are you making?

_____

_____

(Identify the most important conclusions you come to.)

6. What important information are you using to draw your conclusions?

_____

_____

(Here you are looking for facts, experiences, data you are using to support your thinking.)

7. What are the main concepts within your guiding principle? How are key terms for those concepts understood or defined within your guiding principle?

_____

_____

(To identify these, ask yourself: "What are the most important ideas that I need to understand in order to grasp the importance of my guiding principle?")

8. What are the major points of view about your guiding principle? What perspectives do you need to consider?

_____

_____

(What is your worldview? What frames of reference affect your thinking about your guiding principle?)

Part 4 - Change Your Protagonist

According to Drs. Richard Paul and Linda Elder, there is an intimate, dynamic interrelation between thinking, feeling, and wanting. Our minds are continually communicating three kinds of things to us: what is going on in life, feelings (positive or negative) about those events, and things to pursue and where to put our energy (our desires). But our feelings and desires are only changed through our thinking. Therefore, this part works best in conjunction with Practical Step 2 from this chapter: Seek God First.

Now that you've discovered your protagonists (from Part 2) and have a better understanding of the logic behind them (from Part 3), now you can work to make God the main character of your life.

When making a decision take the following actions:

- Notice what is motivating you to do what you are about to do—is it one of the guiding principles you discovered in Part 1?

- Remember what you learned in Step 2 about Seeking God First. Put Step 2 into practice in this case, and discover what God would have you to do.

- Instead of making your decision based on your guiding principle (even if it's a good principle), collaborate with God about what you should do in this case. In this way, you will be actively making God the protagonist of your life!

- Document your progress of focusing your decision-making process on God.

HELPFUL RESOURCES

- Bible Gateway - this website includes dozens of versions of the Bible for you to read for free, as well as other study tools.

- The Bible Project - BibleProject is a nonprofit, crowdfunded organization that produces 100% free Bible videos, podcasts, blogs, classes, and educational Bible resources to help make the biblical story accessible to everyone everywhere.

- Foundation for Critical Thinking - this organization has many useful recourses for intentionally strengthening your own thinking. Some of our favorites are *The Miniature Guide for Critical Thinking: Concepts & Tools*, *The Thinker's Guide to Analytical Thinking,* and *The Thinker's Guide to the Human Mind.*

- Life.Church - this Christian organization provides many online resources including videos, podcasts, devotionals, activities, and other curriculum to help strengthen your relationship with God.

- Study Bibles - study Bibles are really useful because they include definitions, and historical and cultural information that will help you better understand the context of the text you're reading. We recommend the NLT Life Application Study Bible, the ESV Study Bible, and the NIV Cultural Background Study Bible.

More Notes

More Notes

www.ingramcontent.com/pod-product-compliance
Lightning Source LLC
Chambersburg PA
CBHW081005120626
46546CB00010B/3023